Travel journal

My trip to:

_____

If lost please return to:

Name: _____

Phone: _____

Email: _____

Things to do before I go...

- [ ] _____
- [ ] _____
- [ ] _____
- [ ] _____
- [ ] _____
- [ ] _____
- [ ] _____
- [ ] _____
- [ ] _____
- [ ] _____
- [ ] _____
- [ ] _____
- [ ] _____
- [ ] _____
- [ ] _____
- [ ] _____
- [ ] _____
- [ ] _____
- [ ] _____

Flight, Hotels, Car Rental Info...

_____

_____

_____

_____

_____

_____

Packing List

_____

_____

_____

_____

_____

_____

_____

_____

_____

_____

_____

One my trip I would like to...

_____

_____

_____

_____

_____

_____

_____

Basic Foreign word/phrases...

_____

_____

_____

_____

_____

_____

_____

Daily Travel Journal

Date/City/Weather

_____

_____

_____

Places I am planning to visit Today

_____

_____

_____

_____

_____

What to pack in my backpack

_____

_____

_____

_____

Best places I visited Today

_____

_____

_____

My favorite local meal

_____

_____

_____

_____

My favorite part of the day

_____

_____

_____

_____

New words I learned Today

_____

_____

_____

Notes/Funny memories/Anecdotes

_____

_____

_____

_____

_____

_____

_____

_____

Daily Travel Journal

Date/City/Weather

_____

_____

_____

Places I am planning to visit Today

_____

_____

_____

_____

What to pack in my backpack

_____

_____

_____

_____

Best places I visited Today

_____

_____

_____

My favorite local meal

_____

_____

_____

_____

My favorite part of the day

_____

_____

_____

_____

New words I learned Today

_____

_____

_____

Notes/Funny memories/Anecdotes

_____

_____

_____

_____

_____

_____

_____

_____

_____

Daily Travel Journal

Date/City/Weather

_____

_____

_____

Places I am planning to visit Today

_____

_____

_____

_____

_____

What to pack in my backpack

_____

_____

_____

_____

Best places I visited Today

_____

_____

_____

My favorite local meal

_____

_____

_____

_____

My favorite part of the day

_____

_____

_____

_____

New words I learned Today

_____

_____

_____

Notes/Funny memories/Anecdotes

_____

_____

_____

_____

_____

_____

_____

_____

_____

Daily Travel Journal

Date/City/Weather

_____

_____

_____

Places I am planning to visit Today

_____

_____

_____

_____

What to pack in my backpack

_____

_____

_____

_____

Best places I visited Today

_____

_____

_____

My favorite local meal

_____

_____

_____

_____

My favorite part of the day

_____

_____

_____

_____

New words I learned Today

_____

_____

_____

Notes/Funny memories/Anecdotes

_____

_____

_____

_____

_____

_____

_____

_____

_____

_____

Daily Travel Journal

Date/City/Weather

_____

_____

_____

Places I am planning to visit Today

_____

_____

_____

_____

_____

What to pack in my backpack

_____

_____

_____

_____

Best places I visited Today

_____

_____

_____

My favorite local meal

_____

_____

_____

_____

My favorite part of the day

_____

_____

_____

_____

New words I learned Today

_____

_____

_____

Notes/Funny memories/Anecdotes

_____

_____

_____

_____

_____

_____

_____

_____

_____

Daily Travel Journal

Date/City/Weather

_____

_____

_____

Places I am planning to visit Today

_____

_____

_____

_____

What to pack in my backpack

_____

_____

_____

_____

Best places I visited Today

_____

_____

_____

My favorite local meal

_____

_____

_____

_____

My favorite part of the day

_____

_____

_____

_____

New words I learned Today

_____

_____

_____

Notes/Funny memories/Anecdotes

_____

_____

_____

_____

_____

_____

_____

_____

_____

_____

Daily Travel Journal

Date/City/Weather

_____

_____

_____

Places I am planning to visit Today

_____

_____

_____

_____

What to pack in my backpack

_____

_____

_____

_____

Best places I visited Today

_____

_____

_____

My favorite local meal

_____

_____

_____

_____

My favorite part of the day

_____

_____

_____

_____

New words I learned Today

_____

_____

_____

Notes/Funny memories/Anecdotes

_____

_____

_____

_____

_____

_____

_____

_____

_____

Daily Travel Journal

Date/City/Weather

_____

_____

_____

Places I am planning to visit Today

_____

_____

_____

What to pack in my backpack

_____

_____

_____

_____

Best places I visited Today

_____

_____

_____

My favorite local meal

_____

_____

_____

_____

_____

My favorite part of the day

_____

_____

_____

_____

New words I learned Today

_____

_____

_____

Notes/Funny memories/Anecdotes

_____

_____

_____

_____

_____

_____

_____

_____

_____

Daily Travel Journal

Date/City/Weather

_____

_____

_____

Places I am planning to visit Today

_____

_____

_____

_____

What to pack in my backpack

_____

_____

_____

_____

Best places I visited Today

_____

_____

_____

My favorite local meal

_____

_____

_____

_____

My favorite part of the day

_____

_____

_____

_____

New words I learned Today

_____

_____

_____

Notes/Funny memories/Anecdotes

_____

_____

_____

_____

_____

_____

_____

_____

_____

Daily Travel Journal

Date/City/Weather

_____

_____

_____

Places I am planning to visit Today

_____

_____

_____

_____

_____

What to pack in my backpack

_____

_____

_____

_____

Best places I visited Today

_____

_____

_____

My favorite local meal

_____

_____

_____

_____

_____

My favorite part of the day

_____

_____

_____

_____

New words I learned Today

_____

_____

_____

Notes/Funny memories/Anecdotes

_____

_____

_____

_____

_____

_____

_____

_____

_____

Daily Travel Journal

Date/City/Weather

_____

_____

_____

Places I am planning to visit Today

_____

_____

_____

_____

What to pack in my backpack

_____

_____

_____

_____

Best places I visited Today

_____

_____

_____

My favorite local meal

_____

_____

_____

_____

My favorite part of the day

_____

_____

_____

_____

New words I learned Today

_____

_____

_____

Notes/Funny memories/Anecdotes

_____

_____

_____

_____

_____

_____

_____

_____

_____

Daily Travel Journal

Date/City/Weather

_____

_____

_____

Places I am planning to visit Today

_____

_____

_____

_____

What to pack in my backpack

_____

_____

_____

_____

Best places I visited Today

_____

_____

_____

My favorite local meal

_____

_____

_____

_____

My favorite part of the day

_____

_____

_____

_____

New words I learned Today

_____

_____

_____

Notes/Funny memories/Anecdotes

_____

_____

_____

_____

_____

_____

_____

_____

_____

Daily Travel Journal

Date/City/Weather

_____

_____

_____

Places I am planning to visit Today

_____

_____

_____

_____

_____

What to pack in my backpack

_____

_____

_____

_____

Best places I visited Today

_____

_____

_____

My favorite local meal

_____

_____

_____

_____

My favorite part of the day

_____

_____

_____

_____

New words I learned Today

_____

_____

_____

Notes/Funny memories/Anecdotes

_____

_____

_____

_____

_____

_____

_____

_____

_____

Daily Travel Journal

Date/City/Weather

_____

_____

_____

Places I am planning to visit Today

_____

_____

_____

_____

_____

What to pack in my backpack

_____

_____

_____

_____

Best places I visited Today

_____

_____

_____

My favorite local meal

_____

_____

_____

_____

_____

My favorite part of the day

_____

_____

_____

_____

New words I learned Today

_____

_____

_____

Notes/Funny memories/Anecdotes

_____

_____

_____

_____

_____

_____

_____

_____

_____

Daily Travel Journal

Date/City/Weather

_____

_____

_____

Places I am planning to visit Today

_____

_____

_____

_____

_____

What to pack in my backpack

_____

_____

_____

_____

Best places I visited Today

_____

_____

_____

My favorite local meal

_____

_____

_____

_____

My favorite part of the day

_____

_____

_____

_____

New words I learned Today

_____

_____

_____

Notes/Funny memories/Anecdotes

_____

_____

_____

_____

_____

_____

_____

_____

_____

Daily Travel Journal

Date/City/Weather

_____

_____

_____

Places I am planning to visit Today

_____

_____

_____

_____

What to pack in my backpack

_____

_____

_____

_____

Best places I visited Today

_____

_____

_____

My favorite local meal

_____

_____

_____

_____

My favorite part of the day

_____

_____

_____

_____

New words I learned Today

_____

_____

_____

Notes/Funny memories/Anecdotes

_____

_____

_____

_____

_____

_____

_____

_____

_____

Daily Travel Journal

Date/City/Weather

_____

_____

_____

Places I am planning to visit Today

_____

_____

_____

_____

What to pack in my backpack

_____

_____

_____

_____

Best places I visited Today

_____

_____

_____

My favorite local meal

_____

_____

_____

_____

My favorite part of the day

_____

_____

_____

_____

New words I learned Today

_____

_____

_____

Notes/Funny memories/Anecdotes

_____

_____

_____

_____

_____

_____

_____

_____

_____

Daily Travel Journal

Date/City/Weather

Places I am planning to visit Today

What to pack in my backpack

Best places I visited Today

_____

_____

_____

My favorite local meal

_____

_____

_____

_____

_____

My favorite part of the day

_____

_____

_____

_____

New words I learned Today

_____

_____

_____

Notes/Funny memories/Anecdotes

_____

_____

_____

_____

_____

_____

_____

_____

_____

Daily Travel Journal

Date/City/Weather

_____

_____

_____

Places I am planning to visit Today

_____

_____

_____

_____

_____

What to pack in my backpack

_____

_____

_____

_____

Best places I visited Today

_____

_____

_____

My favorite local meal

_____

_____

_____

_____

My favorite part of the day

_____

_____

_____

_____

New words I learned Today

Notes/Funny memories/Anecdotes

Daily Travel Journal

Date/City/Weather

_____

_____

_____

Places I am planning to visit Today

_____

_____

_____

_____

What to pack in my backpack

_____

_____

_____

_____

Best places I visited Today

_____

_____

_____

My favorite local meal

_____

_____

_____

_____

My favorite part of the day

_____

_____

_____

_____

New words I learned Today

_____

_____

_____

Notes/Funny memories/Anecdotes

_____

_____

_____

_____

_____

_____

_____

_____

_____

_____

Daily Travel Journal

Date/City/Weather

_____

_____

_____

Places I am planning to visit Today

_____

_____

_____

_____

What to pack in my backpack

_____

_____

_____

_____

Best places I visited Today

_____

_____

_____

My favorite local meal

_____

_____

_____

_____

_____

My favorite part of the day

_____

_____

_____

_____

New words I learned Today

_____

_____

_____

Notes/Funny memories/Anecdotes

_____

_____

_____

_____

_____

_____

_____

_____

_____

Daily Travel Journal

Date/City/Weather

_____

_____

_____

Places I am planning to visit Today

_____

_____

_____

_____

What to pack in my backpack

_____

_____

_____

_____

Best places I visited Today

_____

_____

_____

My favorite local meal

_____

_____

_____

_____

My favorite part of the day

_____

_____

_____

_____

New words I learned Today

_____

_____

_____

Notes/Funny memories/Anecdotes

_____

_____

_____

_____

_____

_____

_____

_____

_____

Daily Travel Journal

Date/City/Weather

_____

_____

_____

Places I am planning to visit Today

_____

_____

_____

_____

_____

What to pack in my backpack

_____

_____

_____

_____

Best places I visited Today

_____

_____

_____

My favorite local meal

_____

_____

_____

_____

My favorite part of the day

_____

_____

_____

_____

New words I learned Today

_____

_____

_____

Notes/Funny memories/Anecdotes

_____

_____

_____

_____

_____

_____

_____

_____

_____

Daily Travel Journal

Date/City/Weather

_____

_____

_____

Places I am planning to visit Today

_____

_____

_____

_____

What to pack in my backpack

_____

_____

_____

_____

Best places I visited Today

_____

_____

_____

My favorite local meal

_____

_____

_____

_____

My favorite part of the day

_____

_____

_____

_____

New words I learned Today

_____

_____

_____

Notes/Funny memories/Anecdotes

_____

_____

_____

_____

_____

_____

_____

_____

_____

_____

Daily Travel Journal

Date/City/Weather

_____

_____

_____

Places I am planning to visit Today

_____

_____

_____

_____

What to pack in my backpack

_____

_____

_____

_____

Best places I visited Today

_____

_____

_____

My favorite local meal

_____

_____

_____

_____

My favorite part of the day

_____

_____

_____

_____

New words I learned Today

_____

_____

_____

Notes/Funny memories/Anecdotes

_____

_____

_____

_____

_____

_____

_____

_____

_____

Daily Travel Journal

Date/City/Weather

_____

_____

_____

Places I am planning to visit Today

_____

_____

_____

_____

What to pack in my backpack

_____

_____

_____

_____

Best places I visited Today

_____

_____

_____

My favorite local meal

_____

_____

_____

_____

My favorite part of the day

_____

_____

_____

_____

New words I learned Today

_____

_____

_____

Notes/Funny memories/Anecdotes

_____

_____

_____

_____

_____

_____

_____

_____

_____

Daily Travel Journal

Date/City/Weather

_____

_____

_____

Places I am planning to visit Today

_____

_____

_____

_____

What to pack in my backpack

_____

_____

_____

_____

Best places I visited Today

_____

_____

_____

My favorite local meal

_____

_____

_____

_____

My favorite part of the day

_____

_____

_____

_____

New words I learned Today

_____

_____

_____

Notes/Funny memories/Anecdotes

_____

_____

_____

_____

_____

_____

_____

_____

_____

_____

Daily Travel Journal

Date/City/Weather

_____

_____

_____

Places I am planning to visit Today

_____

_____

_____

_____

What to pack in my backpack

_____

_____

_____

_____

Best places I visited Today

_____

_____

_____

My favorite local meal

_____

_____

_____

_____

My favorite part of the day

_____

_____

_____

_____

New words I learned Today

_____

_____

_____

Notes/Funny memories/Anecdotes

_____

_____

_____

_____

_____

_____

_____

_____

_____

Daily Travel Journal

Date/City/Weather

_____

_____

_____

Places I am planning to visit Today

_____

_____

_____

_____

What to pack in my backpack

_____

_____

_____

Best places I visited Today

_____

_____

_____

My favorite local meal

_____

_____

_____

_____

_____

My favorite part of the day

_____

_____

_____

_____

New words I learned Today

_____

_____

_____

Notes/Funny memories/Anecdotes

_____

_____

_____

_____

_____

_____

_____

_____

_____

Daily Travel Journal

Date/City/Weather

_____

_____

_____

Places I am planning to visit Today

_____

_____

_____

_____

What to pack in my backpack

_____

_____

_____

_____

Best places I visited Today

_____

_____

_____

My favorite local meal

_____

_____

_____

_____

My favorite part of the day

_____

_____

_____

_____

New words I learned Today

_____

_____

_____

Notes/Funny memories/Anecdotes

_____

_____

_____

_____

_____

_____

_____

_____

_____

Daily Travel Journal

Date/City/Weather

_____

_____

_____

Places I am planning to visit Today

_____

_____

_____

_____

_____

What to pack in my backpack

_____

_____

_____

_____

Best places I visited Today

_____

_____

_____

My favorite local meal

_____

_____

_____

_____

_____

My favorite part of the day

_____

_____

_____

_____

New words I learned Today

_____

_____

_____

Notes/Funny memories/Anecdotes

_____

_____

_____

_____

_____

_____

_____

_____

_____

_____

Daily Travel Journal

Date/City/Weather

_____

_____

_____

Places I am planning to visit Today

_____

_____

_____

_____

What to pack in my backpack

_____

_____

_____

_____

Best places I visited Today

_____

_____

_____

My favorite local meal

_____

_____

_____

_____

My favorite part of the day

_____

_____

_____

_____

New words I learned Today

_____

_____

_____

Notes/Funny memories/Anecdotes

_____

_____

_____

_____

_____

_____

_____

_____

_____

Daily Travel Journal

Date/City/Weather

_____

_____

_____

Places I am planning to visit Today

_____

_____

_____

_____

What to pack in my backpack

_____

_____

_____

_____

Best places I visited Today

_____

_____

_____

My favorite local meal

_____

_____

_____

_____

My favorite part of the day

_____

_____

_____

_____

New words I learned Today

_____

_____

_____

Notes/Funny memories/Anecdotes

_____

_____

_____

_____

_____

_____

_____

_____

_____

Daily Travel Journal

Date/City/Weather

_____

_____

_____

Places I am planning to visit Today

_____

_____

_____

_____

What to pack in my backpack

_____

_____

_____

_____

Best places I visited Today

_____

_____

_____

My favorite local meal

_____

_____

_____

_____

_____

My favorite part of the day

_____

_____

_____

_____

New words I learned Today

_____

_____

_____

Notes/Funny memories/Anecdotes

_____

_____

_____

_____

_____

_____

_____

_____

_____

Daily Travel Journal

Date/City/Weather

_____

_____

_____

Places I am planning to visit Today

_____

_____

_____

_____

What to pack in my backpack

_____

_____

_____

_____

Best places I visited Today

_____

_____

_____

My favorite local meal

_____

_____

_____

_____

My favorite part of the day

_____

_____

_____

_____

New words I learned Today

_____

_____

_____

Notes/Funny memories/Anecdotes

_____

_____

_____

_____

_____

_____

_____

_____

_____

Daily Travel Journal

Date/City/Weather

_____

_____

_____

Places I am planning to visit Today

_____

_____

_____

_____

What to pack in my backpack

_____

_____

_____

_____

Best places I visited Today

_____

_____

_____

My favorite local meal

_____

_____

_____

_____

My favorite part of the day

_____

_____

_____

_____

New words I learned Today

_____

_____

_____

Notes/Funny memories/Anecdotes

_____

_____

_____

_____

_____

_____

_____

_____

_____

_____

Made in United States
North Haven, CT
16 June 2023

37812415R00069